AGENTS OF ATLAS

Dark Reign

WRITER
Jeff Parker

ARTISTS
Carlo Pagulayan, Jason Paz & Jana Schirmer; Gabriel Hardman
& Elizabeth Dismang; and Clayton Henry & Jana Schirmer

LETTERER
Blambot's Nate Piekos

"THE HEIST"

WRITER
Jeff Parker

ARTISTS
Carlo Pagulayan, Jason Paz & Jana Schirmer

LETTERER
Blambot's Nate Piekos

"WOLVERINE: AGENT OF ATLAS"

WRITER
Jeff Parker

ARTISTS
Benton Jew & Elizabeth Dismang

LETTERER
Blambot's Nate Piekos

"THE RESISTANCE"

WRITER
Jeff Parker

ARTISTS
Leonard Kirk, Karl Kesel & Michelle Madsen

LETTERER
Blambot's Nate Piekos

GIANT SIZE MARVEL ADVENTURES THE AVENGERS #1

WRITER
Jeff Parker

ARTISTS
Leonard Kirk & Val Staples

LETTERER
Dave Sharpe

COVER ARTISTS
Art Adams & Guru eFX; Greg Land & Justin Ponsor; Adi Granov; Stuart Immonen & John Rauch;
Billy Tan & Frank D'Armata; Daniel Acuña; Phil Jimenez, Andy Lanning & Christina Strain;
and Leonard Kirk, Terry Pallot & Chris Sotomayor

ASSISTANT EDITOR
Lauren Sankovitch

ASSOCIATE EDITOR
Nathan Cosby

EDITOR
Mark Paniccia

COLLECTION EDITOR: Cory Levine • EDITORIAL ASSISTANT: Alex Starbuck
ASSISTANT EDITOR: John Denning • EDITORS, SPECIAL PROJECTS: Jennifer Grünwald & Mark D. Beazley
SENIOR EDITOR, SPECIAL PROJECTS: Jeff Youngquist • SENIOR VICE PRESIDENT OF SALES: David Gabriel
PRODUCTION: Jerry Kalinowski • BOOK DESIGN: Spring Hoteling

EDITOR IN CHIEF: Joe Quesada • PUBLISHER: Dan Buckley
EXECUTIVE PRODUCER: Alan Fine

AGENTS of ATLAS: THE HEIST

BUT I DON'T CARE WHO YOU ARE. THIS IS NEAR FIVE THOUSAND TONS OF GOLD INGOTS WE'RE TALKING ABOUT.

AND I'M SURE THAT'S A HONEY OF A FLYING SAUCER YOU'VE GOT UP THERE--MAYBE YOU STOLE IT FROM THE SKRULLS-- BUT IT DOESN'T LOOK LIKE IT CAN CARRY AWAY THAT MUCH PRECIOUS METAL.

I BET EVEN A CHUNK OF IT WOULD SLOW YOU DOWN ENOUGH FOR US TO SHOOT YOU DOWN BEFORE YOU CROSS THE BORDER.

THE GENERAL HAS A POINT, BOB. HOW DO WE PLAN TO TRANSPORT THIS MUCH BULLION?

THAT IS WHAT I AM ARRANGING NOW, MASTER WOO.

AS I MADE THE ROOF INTANGIBLE, I CAN TEMPORARILY ALTER THE ATOMIC STRUCTURE OF THE GOLD TO REDUCE ITS GRAVITY.

I SENSE THE GENERAL NOW FEARS WE'LL BE TAKING SOME OF HIS ARMAMENT. HE CAN RELAX. THIS PROCESS WOULD RENDER COMPLEX MACHINERY UNUSABLE.

IT WILL DEGRADE THE U.S. TREASURY DEMARCATIONS STAMPED INTO THE INGOTS THOUGH.

≥Tssk≤ ARE WE ON SCHEDULE, MR. HALE?

LITTLE BIT AHEAD, IN FACT.

I-I DIDN'T THINK YOU'D NEED ME IN THIS CLOSE, MR. MARKO! CAN I STAY BACK IN THE TRUCK?

THEY USED TO CALL ME MAN-MOUNTAIN. I WAS JUST A HIGH-POWERED THUG IN AND OUT OF JAIL, USUALLY WITH A FACE FULL OF WEBS.

BUT NORMAN OSBORN SEES POTENTIAL, JASON. NOW THIS WHOLE UNIT OF THE ATF ANSWERS TO ME.

OF COURSE, WE DON'T CARE SO MUCH ABOUT THE ALCOHOL AND TOBACCO ANYMORE...

...

...JUST THE FIREARMS.

GROW SOME, JASON, YOU'RE UNDER FEDERAL PROTECTION NOW.

IF THIS PUTS US ONTO WOO'S TEAM, UNCLE SAM IS GOING TO TAKE GOOD CARE OF YOU. JUST LIKE WITH ME.

EUREKA, CALIFORNIA.

HALT! NO ONE ENTERS THIS FACILITY WITHOUT-- AHK--

FEDERAL AGENTS...WE HAVE REASON TO BELIEVE YOU HAVE SOME SERIOUS ARTILLERY IN THERE.

P-TOT

ZZAP

SIR! THE TRUCK WITH THE BATTERING RIG IS READY TO PROCEED.

SAVE IT, ARNETT.

JEFF PARKER - WRITER   CARLO PAGULAYAN - PENCILER   JASON PAZ - INKER

JANA SCHIRMER - COLORIST   BLAMBOT'S NATE PIEKOS - LETTERER   ART ADAMS & GURU eFX - COVER

LAUREN SANKOVITCH - ASSISTANT EDITOR   NATHAN COSBY - ASSOCIATE EDITOR

MARK PANICCIA - EDITOR   JOE QUESADA - EDITOR IN CHIEF   DAN BUCKLEY - PUBLISHER

BOOM **BOOM** **BOOOM**

Oh, *THERE* YOU ARE!

KREEEEENK

CONGRATULATIONS, VENUS. MY BOY IS UNDER YOUR THUMB, LIKE ALL MEN.

I ASSUME THAT SAUCER IS ON THE WAY TO START FIRING ON THE TOWER?

NOT AT ALL. I JUST WANT A MOMENT OF YOUR TIME.

YOU HAVE IT, BUT DON'T WASTE ALL THE CHARM ON ME.

NO MATTER WHAT YOU SAY, HE WON'T HARM ME. AND I'VE GOT INHIBITORS NOW, LISTENING TO A DISTORTION RELAY OF YOUR VOICE.

YOU SOUND HORRIBLE.

Oh POO. SO YOU KNOW WHO I AM?

KHANATA, DEREK

Oh YEAH. I FOUND ALL KINDS OF USEFUL INFO FROM CONFISCATED S.H.I.E.L.D. FILES.

AN AGENT *KHANATA* DID A THOROUGH DOSSIER ON YOU BEFORE YOUR APPARENT "DEMISE."

WOO, JAMES

YOUR MASTER WAS THEN KNOWN AS SUBDIRECTOR JAMES WOO. GOT HIMSELF IN CRITICAL CONDITION TRYING TO RAID THE LAIR OF HIS OLD ENEMY, THE YELLOW CLAW.

ROBERT GRAYSON Alias: MARVEL BOY

KEN HALE Alias: GORILLA MAN

M-11 (The Human Robot)

BUT HIS OLD COMRADES FROM HIS DAYS IN THE FBI REMEMBERED HIM, AND CAME BACK FOR HIM.

BOB GRAYSON USED HIS URANIAN TECHNOLOGY TO RESTORE WOO--SNAPPED HIM RIGHT BACK TO HIS TWENTIES.

I'D LIKE THAT MYSELF.

KHANATA EARNED THE TEAM'S TRUST BY LEADING THEM TO YOU IN AFRICA.

THEN YOU DRAFTED A REAL HEAVY HITTER--

NAMORA OF ATLANTIS. NICE.

THE LAST THING KHANATA'S JOURNALS HAVE IS YOU ALL DYING IN ANOTHER RAID ON THE ATLAS FOUNDATION'S SECRET LAIR--OBVIOUSLY B.S., SINCE NAMORA STARTED POPPING UP DURING HULK'S INVASION.

BUT SOMEHOW YOU ALL WENT FROM TRYING TO CRUSH ATLAS TO RUNNING THE SHOW.

ALL MAKE ROOM FOR HIS MAJESTY--WOO YEN JET, RULER OF THE ATLAS FOUNDATION!

SOUNDS LIKE QUITE A SWITCH TO ME. HELL, I'D THINK THAT WAS THE YELLOW CLAW HIMSELF.

AND THEN OF COURSE, HE SENDS THE DEADLIEST OF HIS BUNCH HERE TO MEET WITH ME.

YOU WERE REAL HONEST-TO-GO MYTHICAL BEAST...A SIR LURING SAILORS WATERY GRAVES, T WHOLE WORL

YOUR BODY COUNT ALON EQUALS THAT OF A SMALL WAR.

REALLY, THE OTHERS ARE LIGHTWEIGHTS COMPARED TO YOU.

I MEAN, WE KNOW YOU'RE NO GODDESS OF LOVE, RIGHT?

SOME SORCERER CURSED YOU WITH THE ABILITY TO HAVE A SOUL, AND YOU SPENT A CENTURY BLOCKING ALL THAT OUT-- THE SHEER SCOPE OF IT WAS TOO MUCH.

BUT CHANGE DOESN'T ALWAYS STICK, HUH?

BELIEVE ME, BEAUTIFUL, I KNOW IT.

IMPRESSIVE, MR. OSBORN. YOU ARE AS ON TOP OF THINGS AS WE HAD HEARD. THAT'S WHY WE WANT TO OPEN A DIALOGUE WITH YOU.

BY ALL MEANS. I AM NOTHING IF NOT A NETWORKER.

GOOD. THEN I INTRODUCE...

YOUR TOUR WILL GIVE YOU A CLEAR IDEA OF OUR VAST RESOURCES AND INFLUENCE, BUT KEEP IN MIND...

THERE ARE ARCANE MAGICS AND SCIENCES AT WORK EVERYWHERE IN THE HIDDEN CITY. SHOULD YOU VEER FROM THE PATH, YOUR SAFETY CANNOT BE GUARANTEED.

FIRST, THE CONCLAVE OF WARRIOR SCHOLARS. THEY ARE LARGELY RESPONSIBLE IN ESTABLISHING BUSINESS FRONTS FOR ATLAS OPERATIONS.

NO, PLEASE! YOU DON'T KNOW WHAT THEY'LL DO TO ME!

IT'S BEEN GREAT, JASON.

AS IT HAS ALWAYS BEEN, ATLAS HAS HAD GREAT SUCCESS WITH HIDING IN PLAIN SIGHT.

OUR UBIQUITOUS NAME MAKES IT EASY FOR OUR MINIONS TO INTERACT WITH VARIOUS HOLDINGS WHILE COMMITTING NO EVIDENCE TO RECORD...

MARKO, WHAT ARE YOU DOING?!

PLEASE! NO ONE ELSE STRAY FROM THE PATH!

KNEW IT.

ALL RIGHT, JASON--YOU BETTER COME CLEAN. I *THOUGHT* YOU WEREN'T IN ANY DANGER.

HOW D-DID YOU KNOW?

EVERYBODY THINKS 'CAUSE I'M BIG I CAN'T BE SMART. I'M NO EINSTEIN, BUT I PUT SOMETHING TOGETHER.

ATLAS IS SO BAD, YET THEY DIDN'T KILL ANY OF MY MEN?

AND THEY SHOULD HAVE FOUND YOU THE OTHER NIGHT--THAT ROBOT WAS THROWING OUR TRUCKS AROUND, BUT SOMEHOW YOU'RE HIDDEN SAFELY IN ONE WHEN THEY DUMPED US IN THE DESERT.

YOU GOT ME THERE, BIG GUY.

ALL RIGHT, BOB, DROP MY COVER.

TALK ABOUT PICKING A CRAP TIME TO SUDDENLY GET SMART.

WHAT...? HEY...

HE HAD NO USEFUL KNOWLEDGE, AND YOU SQUANDERED A CHANCE TO BRING THE SENTRY HERE UNDER OUR CONTROL. I FEAR YOUR MISSIONS ARE NOT FURTHERING THE GOALS OF THE KHAN DYNASTY AS YOU VOWED...

...TO RETURN THE EMPIRE TO GREATNESS UNDER A UNITED WORLD.

I BELIEVE WE CAN DO BOTH, LAO. YOUR *ADVICE* IS UNDER CONSIDERATION.

THANK YOU, *MASTER* WOO...BUT THIS NEW WORLD ORDER IS EVEN MORE DANGEROUS TH WHAT YOUR PREDECESSOR HAD TO DEAL WIT AND YOU INSIST ON PUTTING YOURSELF ON THE FRONT LINE.

SO I HAVE SENT A TEAM FROM THE ROYAL COUNCIL TO THE EAST TO ACTIVATE A *SECOND*, WHO CAN TAKE YOUR PLACE SHOULD... TRAGEDY BEFALL YOU.

A SECOND? UNDER WHAT AUTHORITY?

THE BYLAWS ARE CLEARLY WRITTEN ON THE EAST WALL, MY DEAR.

UNTIL JAM PICKS A QUALIFI SUCCESSOR--IN T FAR FUTURE, ONE HOPES IT IS MY PREROGATIVE APPOINT A BACKI

WE'LL TAKE THIS UP LATER.

BOB, THANKS--I KNOW YOU'RE BEAT FROM HOLDING THAT PROJECTION FOR SO LONG.

JUST A WEEK WITHOUT SLEEP. I HOPE THE OPERATION WORKED.

WE'LL KNOW TOMORROW. M-11 WILL TAKE THE ENVOY BACK TO THE DESERT, YOU GET SOME REST.

THE REPORT WAS AS GLOWING AS I'D HOPED, MR. WOO.

EXCEPT FOR THE BIT ABOUT MARKO WANDERING OFF INTO A MONSTER PIT? DAMN, CAN'T A MAN GO TAKE A LEAK THERE?

ALLIES ARE A GOOD THING. I'LL BE IN TOUCH SOON.

WVIP

HE WAS WARNED. I AM HAPPY THAT WE WILL BE WORKING TOGETHER.

DO YOU TRUST HIM?

TRUST? OH HELL NO.

BUT WE HAVE A GOOD BALANCE OF POWER THAT WILL SERVE US BOTH. THAT'S *BETTER* THAN TRUST, VICTORIA.

REMINDS ME, I NEED TO GET THIS PLACE FITTED WITH SONIC DAMPENERS AND HOOK REYNOLDS UP WITH SOME EXPENSIVE EARPLUGS.

HAMMER

WOO, JAMES

ENHANCING...

WHAT IF WOO'S AMBITION GROWS?

I'VE READ UP ON HIM.

WOO YEN JET MAY FANCY HIMSELF THE LEADER OF AN UNDERGROUND EMPIRE, BUT THAT'S NOT WHERE HE COMES FROM.

I'M THINKING A BIG PART OF HIM IS STILL JUST A BRASSY KID OUT OF THE 1950s.

JIMMY WOO, UNDERCOVER AGENT.

HEY! THE ATF GUYS ARE GETTING CLOSE TO OUR MEET POINT. WHY OUT HERE BY EDWARDS?

OSBORN WANTS TO REMIND US THAT HE HAS THE MILITARY IN HIS POCKET NOW.

GEEZ, HE MUST'VE SOLD CONGRESS A SERIOUS BILL OF GOODS.

NOW IT'S OUR TURN TO SELL SOMETHING TO HIM. KEEP US INVISIBLE, WE HAVE TO MAKE AN IMPRESSION.

WHO'S THE BIG PIMP, VENUS?

THAT'S MAX MARKHAM, FORMERLY KNOWN AS "GRIZZLY." I GUESS NORMAN OSBORN WANTS THAT ATF DIVISION LED BY WALL-SMASHING TYPES.

WHERE'S BOB WITH THAT CANNON?

BwOOP BwOOP

BwOOP

JAMES, I SEE YOU AGAIN ACCOMPANY YOUR INNER CIRCLE ON A FIELD MISSION--NOT THAT YOU EVER NEED TO...

WE'RE TRYING TO CLOSE A DEAL, MR. LAO. I WANT TO BE ON SITE TO ADVISE.

YOU CAN EASILY OBSERVE AND COMMENT FROM THE HIDDEN CITY, JUST AS I DO NOW.

I LIKE TO GET SOME FRESH AIR NOW AND THEN, AND SAY, AREN'T I THE KHAN? BECAUSE LAST TIME I LOOKED EVERYONE WAS BOWING TO ME.

IN YOUR FACE, SCALES.

NO ONE DISPUTES YOUR RULE.

BUT IT IS YOUR INSISTENCE ON OPERATING IN THE FIELD THAT FORCED ME TO INVOKE THE APPOINTMENT OF YOUR SECOND.

WHO, BY THE WAY, HAS NOW ARRIVED AND AWAITS YOU.

GOOD.

MAKE HIM SOME TEA AND QUIT BUGGING ME. WE'LL BE BACK AFTER THIS DEAL IS CLOSED.

BLEEP

OKAY, GANG. IT'S FUN MAKING THE ATF COOL THEIR HEELS BUT WE'VE GOT STUFF TO DO.

VENUS, CAN YOU GO SEE WHAT THE HOLDUP IS WITH BOB?

I'M GOING IN.

FORCE BUBBLE...SET TO OXYGEN/ NITROGEN...

AND I ENTER THE VIRTUAL BOWELS OF URANUS.

EWWW.

EDWARDS AIR FORCE BASE, ANTELOPE VALLEY--CALIFORNIA.

1958.

BOOM

THERE-- SEE? THERE IT IS!

EVERY OTHER DAY WE HEAR THE SONIC BOOM AND THAT SOVIET MIG APPEARS--IT RACES AROUND THE DESERT FOR A FEW MINUTES THEN DISAPPEARS WITH ANOTHER BOOM.

WHY DON'T YOU SHOOT IT DOWN, MAJOR GARLAND?

WE'VE TRIED, GORILLA MAN, BUT IT APPEARS IN A DIFFERENT PLACE EVERY TIME. ALL FAR ENOUGH AWAY FROM OUR INSTALLATIONS THAT IF THEY'RE SPYING, THEY'RE DOING A LOUSY JOB.

BOB, THINK YOU CAN CATCH UP TO IT AND HAVE A LOOK-SEE?

BOY CAN I--ALL THE SUN OUT HERE HAS MY BANDS CHARGED UP TO BURSTING!

YOUR MYSTERY PILOT IS GOING TO FIND OUT WHY THEY CALL ME--

MARVEL BOYYYY!

STAY SUB-SONIC JUST A MINUTE LONGER...

"YET I CAN STILL REMEMBER YOU BLASTING THROUGH THE SUNNY SKY AS CLEAR AS IF IT WERE THIS MORNING."

WON'T LOSE ME THAT EASY!

I'VE GOT YOU NOW!

SAY, PHANTOM PILOT, GOING MY--

...WAY...?

"LIGHT REFRACTION OFF, BECOMING VISIBLE..."

NOW.

VMMMMMMMM

AHH!

WHAT THE--?!

ALL RIGHT, LADIES, ON BEHALF OF THE GOVERNMENT TRY NOT TO LOOK ALL RATTLED, HUH?

LOOK AT THIS FREAK SHOW. THIS IS OUR ARMS SUPPLIER?

NOT TO OVERSTEP, MAX, BUT ALL WE'VE GOT OF YOUR PREDECESSOR IS A TORN PIECE OF JACKET WITH TEETH MARKS.

SOME DIPLOMACY, I'M SAYING.

HOWDY.

I'LL CUT TO THE CHASE, EVERYBODY'S GOT WORK TO DO.

WHAT YOU GENTS ARE LOOKING AT HERE IS TECHNOLOGY FROM AN ADVANCED CIVILIZATION THAT NO LONGER EXISTS. THIS FREQUENCY CANNON WAS PRODUCED IN THE ONLY URANIAN WEAPONS LAB STILL OPERATING.

M-11?

IT PRODUCES THE EFFECT OF AN ELECTROMAGNETIC PULSE, BUT THE PROBLEM WITH AN E.M.P. IS IT TENDS TO FRY ALL *YOUR* EQUIPMENT TOO.

THIS CANNON AFFECTS ONLY WHAT YOU FIRE AT, AND NO AMOUNT OF EARTH-MADE INSULATION OR SAFEGUARDS CAN STOP IT FROM SHUTTING DOWN ITS TARGET. EVEN CHEMICAL COMBUSTION IS KIBOSHED.

DID YOU HEAR ME? DID YOU HEAR ME?!

AAK!

GETMEOUT-- GETMEOUT--

YO, NEPTUNA, WHOA-WHOA!

HEY, WHAT'S GOING ON DOWN THERE?

I THINK I KNOW, I'LL TALK TO HER LATER.

WELL, SHE'S GOING TO KILL THOSE GUYS NOW!

M-11, GET HER OFF 'EM!

GET BACK, M-11, I'VE--

I'VE GOT TO--

I'VE GOT TO GO INSIDE.

YOU CAN FINISH HERE.

uunhh...

GERROFF ME...

CREEAAK

SEE, GRIZ?

THIS BABY EVEN KEPT THE COPTER FROM EXPLODING WHEN SHE SLAMMED IT ON YOU!

NOW HOW MUCH WOULD YOU PAY?

WE DIDN'T EVEN NEED BOB TO WHIP UP THAT CANNON. I COULDA SOLD THOSE CHUMPS SNOT ROCKETS!

CLINK

YOU'RE THE BEST.

AW, *YEAH!* WHO'S THE NUMBER ONE SALES-APE IN THE BAY AREA?

I GOTTA SAY, THOUGH, WE STARTED GOING OFF-PLAN THERE FOR A BIT--

THE FAULT IS MINE, JIMMY. I REGRET MY LOSS OF CONTROL, IT SHALL NOT HAPPEN AGAIN.

HEY, IT'S NOT A DEAL-BREAKER-- IN FACT, YOU BEING OVER-PROTECTIVE OF M-11 AT THAT MOMENT REALLY SOLD THE THREAT OF THE CANNON.

BUT IF THERE'S ANYTHING YOU WANT TO TAL--

THANK YOU.

I WOULD LIKE TO PUT IT BEHIND US, THEN.

WERE I YOU...

...I WOULD PUT ALL OF THESE ESCAPADES BEHIND AND BEGIN ANEW WITH TRUE PURPOSE.

WHO THE HELL--?

Uh...

IT WAS WEIRD ENOUGH AND THEN YOU HAD TO GET THE SKELETON IN THERE.

HERE'S THE TIMES AND PLACES OF EACH APPEARANCE OUR MEN RECORDED.

CLEAR WHY THE BUREAU PUT YOU IN TOUCH WITH US. BOB WILL CRACK THIS.

EXCUSE ME, AGENT WOO, I'M CARY DEKUM-- EVERYONE CALLS ME KIT.

I KNEW THIS KID WAS GOING TO PIPE UP EVENTUALLY.

MAJOR GARLAND TOLD YOU ABOUT THE MANNED SPACE PROGRAM WE'RE STARTING UP HERE...

SURE.

WELL SIR, I WAS WONDERING... I KNOW IT'S A LOT TO ASK, BUT--

BOB, I THINK THIS PILOT WOULD LIKE TO SEE WHAT IT'S LIKE TO FLY IN THE SILVER BULLET.

Oh?

I THINK THERE'S ROOM FOR ONE MORE.

HOW'S THE RIDE, KIT?

THIS IS... SOMETHING ELSE! AND...

...YOU CAN REALLY GO TO OTHER PLANETS IN THIS?

YES. I FLEW IT HERE FROM...

FROM...?

...THE SEVENTH PLANET. I OFFERED TO TALK TO VON BRAUN ABOUT ROCKETRY, BUT YOUR SUPERIORS HAVE "RUN INTERFERENCE" AS KEN SAYS.

YEAH... THEY'RE A CLOSED SHOP WHEN IT COMES TO WORKING WITH OUTSIDERS. IT'S ALL RED SCARE STUFF, YA KNOW? THEY'RE A METICULOUS BUNCH IN LOTS OF WAYS.

I THINK LETTING ME GO ON LEAVE WITH YOU ALL IS A STEP, FORWARD AT LEAST.

I COULD HAVE THEM ON THE MOON BY NEXT YEAR IF THEY'D THROW ORBS.

PLAY BALL.

WE'LL BE IN THE BAY AREA IN A COUPLE OF MINUTES. YOU CAN WALK AROUND THE CABIN IF YOU WANT.

THANKS!

HELLO, KIT. I WAS WONDERING IF YOU WERE GOING TO COME BACK AND TALK TO *ME*.

AH... HEL-HELLO...

VENUS...

WE LIKE IT BECAUSE NO ONE STARES AT KEN. THEY JUST THINK HE'S WEARING A COSTUME FOR ATMOSPHERE.

I THINK I'VE PREDICTED THE MIG'S NEXT ARRIVAL HERE.

THANKS, MAR--*BOB.* I'LL REPORT THIS BACK TO BASE.

THEY'RE MAINLY KNOWN FOR OYSTERS, BUT I TELL YA IT'S A GOOD SALAD HERE!

I WAS NEVER MUCH INTO IT UNTIL I GOT HAIRY, NOW I WANT THE STUFF ALL THE TIME.

BOB WAS SAYING YOU USED TO FLY PLANES A LOT, MR. HALE.

MOSTLY PONTOON JOBS OUT IN THE ISLANDS, BACK WHEN I WAS WHAT YA'D CALL A SOLDIER OF FORTUNE. NEVER REALLY FOUND MUCH OF THAT "FORTUNE" PART.

BUT HEY-- GUESS WHO CHUCK YEAGER LET TAKE THE BELL-X1 FOR A SPIN A FEW YEARS AGO?

HOLY GEE-- REALLY?

HE OWED ME ONE.

BEST WATCH IT, DAD! THEY CAN ARREST YOU FOR HAVIN' THAT STUFF IN HERE.

THEY CAN?

BUT IT'S JUST DAIRY COW-DERIVED MILK, SOLD IN STORES EVERYWHERE...

THEY'RE PULLING YOUR LEG, BOB. I'LL EXPLAIN IT...

...LATER...

WHAT GIVES, BOSS-MAN? IS THERE... oh!

JIMMY, IS THAT... SUWAN?

EXCUSE ME, V.

I GOT YOUR MESSAGE.

CAN WE GO SOMEWHERE PRIVATE?

HEY, WHERE DID JIMMY GO?

HE SAW HIS OLD SWEETHEART-- HER UNCLE IS THE CRIMINAL MASTERMIND YELLOW CLAW-- MAYBE SHE SNUCK BACK INTO TOWN JUST TO *WOO* JIMMY!

GET IT?

SEE, WE BLEW UP HIS BASE IN MONGOLIA...

CLAW? SO...SHE'S A COMMIE--AND HE'S FRIENDLY WITH HER?

YOU DON'T HAVE TO WORRY ABOUT JIMMY'S LOYALTIES.

POINT YOUR WORRY OVER HERE. BOB, WHAT ARE YOU DOING?

GOT SOME DRINKS LIKE THOSE BEAT FELLOWS --›*GULP*‹--SHOW *THEM* WHO'S SQUARE...

SLOW DOWN, SON, YOU'RE GONNA SWALLOW AN UMBRELLA!

SOMEONE OUGHT TO CHECK ON HIM.

NOW, KIT, GIVE JIMMY HIS PRIVACY. AM I GOING TO HAVE TO BREAK INTO SONG?

YOU...

YOU KNOW WHERE *SHE* IS!

"WE'VE BEEN BREACHED!"

AAHHH!!!

GET AWAY FROM HER, FREAK--

GAAHH!

Whoop-- THE SWEET SOUNDS OF A BAR-FIGHT REVVIN' UP! C'MON, JUNIOR, LET'S GET IN IT!

CRASH

Oh-KAY!

WELL, SWELL.

FLUMP

WATCH OUT, MR. HALE-- DON'T TOUCH THEM!

THEM?

The SALE / The DRAGON'S CORRIDOR PART ONE

WRITER: JEFF PARKER
ARTISTS, PRESENT DAY: CARLO PAGULAYAN, JASON PAZ & JANA SCHIRMER
ARTISTS, 1958: GABRIEL HARDMAN & ELIZABETH DISMANG BREITWEISER
LETTERER: BLAMBOT'S NATE PIEKOS   COVER: LAND & PONSOR
VARIANT COVER: MCGUINNESS, VINES & PONSOR   PRODUCTION: IRENE LEE
ASS'T EDITOR: LAUREN SANKOVITCH   SENIOR EDITOR: MARK PANICCIA
EDITOR IN CHIEF: JOE QUESADA   PUBLISHER: DAN BUCKLEY

1958.

‹WHERE IS THE CHINESE WOMAN?›

‹ANSWER NOW OR WE WILL BURN THIS BUILDING DOWN!›

VMMM

Emm...

...lebbn.

THUMP

HANG ON, I THINK I KNOW WHERE THIS GAL YOU'RE LOOKING FOR IS.

THE DRAGON'S CORRIDOR, PART 2 / INTERLUDE AT SEA

ARTISTS, STORY 1: GABRIEL HARDMAN & ELIZABETH DISMANG   ARTISTS, STORY 2: CLAYTON HENRY & JANA SCHIRMER   LETTERER: BLAMBOT'S NATE PIEKOS
COVER: ADI GRANOV   VARIANT COVER: McGUINNESS, VINES & PONSOR   WOLVERINE VARIANT: GERALD PAREL   PRODUCTION: IRENE LEE
ASST. EDITOR: LAUREN SANKOVITCH   EDITOR: MARK PANICCIA   EDITOR IN CHIEF: JOE QUESADA   PUBLISHER: DAN BUCKLEY   EXEC. PRODUCER: ALAN FINE

COME IN, AGENT ONE! HEY!

WHAT IS IT, KEN?

A BUNCH OF FINKS IN BLACK UNIFORMS ARE SHOOTIN' UP THE PLACE, LOOKING FOR SOME CHINA DOLL!

VENUS CAN'T PULL IT TOGETHER TO SING, AND BOB'S THREE SHEETS TO THE WIND!

HOLY COW!

WHY DID I PARK WAY DOWN HERE? IT'S A BATTLEFIELD UP THERE AND I COULDN'T HEAR IT!

I THINK-- THOSE PEOPLE ARE HERE AFTER ME, JIMMY!

SU, WE'VE GOTTA TALK ABOUT YOUR CAREER CHOICES SOMETIME.

BUT FOR NOW, PLEASE, JUST STAY HERE, OKAY?

JIMMY, VENUS IS OKAY, BUT SHE'S BURNED--

HEY, YOU GOT ANOTHER GUN?

KAKK KAK KAKK

NO!

THIS ONE WILL BE ENOUGH!

KAK KAK KAK

HURRY UP, JIMMY...! THIS MASSAGE IS *NOT* RELAXING!

BLAM BLAM BLAM

FBI! PUT DOWN YOUR WEAPONS!

MASKS, EVERYONE!

PSHHHHHHH

Coff— ohk...

WHAT, DID YOU BOYS FORGET ABOUT--

--ME ≥hahk≤ ≥kaff≤

⟨OF COURSE OUR GAS AFFECTS MONKEYS.⟩

⟨IT WAS TESTED ON THEM!⟩

HA HA!

KLUNK KLUNK

KLUNK KLUNK KLUNK KLUNK

⟨THERE'S ANOTHER!⟩

⟨FIRE!⟩

KAK KAK KRAK

KAK

PING

PING

KAK KAK

PING PING

⟨HE'S STILL COMING!⟩

>Coff<
WHAT--

...'COURSE. THANKS, BIG GUY.

WHEPEPEP

JIMMY, I'M SORRY I DIDN'T HELP, I JUST COULDN'T FOCUS--

IT'S OKAY, V. M-11 TOOK CARE OF IT.

I'LL SAY HE DID.

HOLY--!

CHECK THIS OUT. THE ONLY THINGS THAT M-11'S BEAM DIDN'T VAPORIZE ARE THESE RED TRIANGLES.

THEY MUST BE TOUGH.

LET'S GATHER THEM UP. BOB WILL WANT TO ANALYZE THEM.

THAT KID'S GOING TO BE ANALYZING HIS DINNER FOR A WHILE.

SUWAN!

URRKK...

HEY, I JUST SAW SOMETHING GLOWING THROUGH THIS...

NUTS.

IT'S GONE NOW. THAT WAS WEIRD, LIKE 3-D GLASSES.

I GOTTA CALL THIS IN. YOU CAN ALL HEAD BACK AND HIT THE SACK.

YOU DON'T HAVE TO TELL SPACE BOY, HE'S WAY AHEAD OF US AS USUAL.

YOU DON'T HAVE [T]O SING, VENUS, [I']M NOT GOING [T]O BITE YOUR HEAD OFF.

GOOD. WILL THAT GIANT EEL?

HE'S JUST HERE FOR LIGHT. I'M KICKING UP A LOT OF SILT.

IT'S A WARSHIP, RIGHT?

YOU WOULDN'T BELIEVE HOW MANY WORLD WAR II WRECKS ARE OUT HERE...FILLED WITH DIESEL OIL, CLOSE TO CORRODING OPEN AND SPILLING OUT INTO THE SEA.

THE SAFEST THING TO DO IS DRAIN THEM AND THEN PULL THEM UP.

JIMMY HAS LET ME USE SOME OF ATLAS' SUPER-TANKERS.

KLUNK

WHAT A BIG JOB--

WHY HAVEN'T YOU ASKED ANY OF US TO HELP?

THERE'S ENOUGH TO DO WITH TACKLING OSBORN AND H.A.M.M.E.R.

THE OCEAN IS REALLY MORE MY PROBLEM.

WE'RE SUPPOSED TO BE FIXING THE *WHOLE* WORLD, SO THIS SURELY QUALIFIES.

SEE THAT? IT'S A MUNITIONS SHIP FULL OF MINES THAT CAN *STILL* EXPLODE.

M-11 COULD SURVIVE A CHAIN REACTION FROM THAT, BUT NOT THE REST OF YOU.

PLSHH

FOLLOW ME.

THERE'S A LAVA VENT DOWN IN THIS TRENCH, SO IT GETS WARMER SOON.

I CAN TAKE IT, I WAS A SEA MONSTER, REMEMBER?

I SHOULD NEVER HAVE CALLED YOU THAT.

WELL, IT WAS TRUE. I ACCEPT IT NOW INSTEAD OF TRYING TO FORGET.

WISE.

HERE IT IS.

IT... IT'S BEAUTIFUL. WHEN WAS THIS MADE?

THOSE MONTHS I WENT BACK TO ATLANTIS. THERE WASN'T ANYTHING LEFT OF HER TO ENTOMB, SO I HAD OUR MASTER CARVERS COME HERE TO SCULPT THIS MONUMENT. THE PACIFIC WAS MORE OUR HOME.

I COME DOWN HERE SOMETIMES TO THINK OF HER.

AND WONDER. WHY TRITON BROUGHT ME BACK JUST WHEN NAMORITA WAS TAKEN.

WHY I HAD TO SPEND DECADES UNDER ICE WHEN SHE NEEDED ME.

I COULD HAVE TRAINED HER PROPERLY.

I COULD HAVE KEPT HER AWAY FROM...

...FROM...

I COULD HAVE STOPPED THAT BASTARD FROM BLOWING HER UP...

I COULD HAVE...

YOU DON'T KNOW THAT, THERE'S NO WAY TO KNOW.

WHY... WHY COULDN'T I HAVE SEEN HER ONE LAST TIME...?

WHY...

"MORNING, TEAM. VENUS, HOW'S THAT SHOULDER FEELING?"

BOB'S SPACE GOO HAS PATCHED ME RIGHT UP.

THIS IS A RADIATION BURN, BUT THE DECAY RATE IS MUCH FASTER. SHE'S ALREADY CLEAR.

DON'T WORRY, EVERYBODY. WE CAN DITCH THE DANGEROUS LIFESTYLE AFTER I CALL IN THESE HORSES.

I GOT MY SYSTEM DOWN PAT.

IF YEAGER HERE EVER STOPS CHATTIN' UP THE WHOLE AIR FORCE.

SORRY, MR. HALE. I WAS TELLING EDWARDS CONTROL ABOUT MARVEL BOY'S GUESS FOR THE NEXT APPEARANCE OF THE GHOST MiG.

NOT A GUESS.

BRIING

I'M NEVER GOING TO GET MY BOOKIE IN TIME!

AGENT WOO SPEA-- SUWAN?

YOU'RE-- WAIT, WHERE?

CAN'T TALK, I THINK THEY'RE CLOSE--

DID YOU RECOVER THE TRIANGLES?

YEAH, HOW DID YOU KNOW ABOUT THE TRI--

SUWAN! WHAT'S HAPPENING?!

LET GO!

STAY ON THE LINE!

M-11!

WHERE DID THIS CALL ORIGINATE?

BOOTH 463-- PRESIDIO CEMETERY.

LET'S GO!

BOB, YOU FLY AHEAD AND WE'LL CATCH UP! BRING THOSE TRIANGLES.

4.3 MINUTES LATER.

SORRY, JIMMY, I WAS HERE THIRTY SECONDS AFTER THE CALL--I DON'T KNOW HOW THEY GOT AWAY SO FAST.

I'VE COVERED A SQUARE MILE OUT FROM THIS POINT.

HOW DID THEY CLEAR THAT WITH A HOSTAGE?

JIMMY, LOOK AT THIS!

THERE'S SOME GLOWING SHAPE OVER THERE--BUT ONLY IF YOU LOOK THROUGH THE TRIANGLE!

BOB OR M-11-- ANYBODY GETTING THIS?

YES! IT DOESN'T REGISTER LIKE ANYTHING I'M USED TO.

THOSE TRACKS--SHE WAS DRAGGED INTO IT!

MAYBE BOB CAN SEND A PROBE IN AND TEST FOR--

--OR, WE CAN CHARGE ON THROUGH LIKE A ROBOT.

EVERYBODY TAKE ONE OF THESE, SUWAN MADE THEM SOUND IMPORTANT. ALL RIGHT...

...LET'S SEE WHAT'S ON THE OTHER SIDE.

WELL.

Oh YEAH, *THIS* ANSWERS EVERYTHING.

"YOU WESTERNERS HAVE NO CONCEPT OF *TIME.*"

"...THE FACTORY."

PRODUCTION'S IN HIGH GEAR, GOOD. I ESPECIALLY LIKE THAT THE WHOLE OPERATION IS MANEUVERABLE.

MASTER WOO GOT THE IDEA WHEN YOU, Y'KNOW, BLEW UP ONE OF HIS OTHER FACTORIES.

HERE'S A NEW PROTOTYPE WITH THE PARTICLE BEAM YOU WANTED.

NEED IT. PROTECTING AMERICA TAKES OFFENSE AS WELL AS DEFENSE.

SO WHERE'S WOO? I MEAN HEY, I CAME OUT IN PERSON.

HE HAD TO GO DEAL WITH SOME UPPITY LITTLE COUNTRY.

I KNOW HOW IT IS, I HAVE SOME FIRES TO PUT OUT MYSELF.

LOOKING GOOD, KEEP ME APPRISED WHEN THE FIRST RUN IS READY.

LET'S GO, SENTRY.

Ahh-- OKAY THEN.

BOB, IS THE SHIP SOUNDPROOFED AGAINST GOLDEN BOY?

Y-YES.

MORE UNSETTLING WAS THE SENTRY'S IMPENETRABLE DARKNESS THAT SEEMED TO STRETCH INFINITELY.

I HAD TO CUT OFF RECONNAISSANCE OR...I DON'T KNOW WHAT WOULD HAVE HAPPENED TO ME.

THANKS, BOB...THAT'S A LOT TO CHEW ON.

MAYBE YOU BETTER GO RECOVER IN THE SAUCER, WE'LL TAKE THE SMALL COPTER INTO TOWN.

I AGREE. THANK YOU.

I USED TO THINK READING MINDS WOULD BE A PRETTY ACE SKILL. BUT YOU KNOW, I DON'T REALLY ENVY BOB NOW.

OH HELL NO.

IT'S HARD ENOUGH STAYING IN MY OWN HEAD.

SO NOW WHAT, WE'RE GOING TO DO SOME MORE CLUE-DROPPING?

YEAH, TIME TO BAIT THE HOOK...

IS THAT TEMUGIN DOWN THERE IN THE WATER?

Heh.

YEP. GET THE UNDERWORLD MUMBLING "ATLAS" ALL OVER NEW YORK.

IT'S TRICKY, BUT IF WE TIME IT RIGHT--

SO, WE RILE UP SOME THUGS WITH MORE CASH AND BOGUS ERRANDS?

INCOMING!

THIS PLACE DON'T LOOK OR FEEL RIGHT.

HEY, THE TRIANGLES GLOW HERE.

AN ANCIENT BATTLEFIELD?

THIS IS SOME SUBSECTION OF THE TIME AND SPACE WE KNOW.

SHINING MY LIGHT THROUGH IT...

...I CAN SEE SEVERAL OTHER PORTALS ON THE HORIZON.

THOSE COMMIES COULD HAVE GONE THROUGH ANY OF THEM!

NO, LOOK...

THAT ONE--IT'S SHAPED JUST LIKE THESE EMBLEMS. I BET IT HELPS THOSE AGENTS FIND THEIR WAY BACK TO THEIR BASE.

GOTTA BE LIVELIER THAN THIS PLACE!

THE DRAGON'S CORRIDOR, PART 3

WRITER: JEFF PARKER
ARTIST: GABRIEL HARDMAN
COLORIST: ELIZABETH DISMANG
LETTERER: BLAMBOT'S NATE PIEKOS

〈WE ARE INFILTRATED!〉

〈THEY ARE USING THE CORRIDOR!〉

HEY!

SUWAN!

M-11, PUT THEM DOWN!

ZOOOT

AAHHH!

GET AWAY FROM HER!

JIMMY!

HURRY, I HEAR MORE OF 'EM COMING IN FROM THE WOODS.

PLEASE SAY YOU ALL CARRIED THE EMBLEMS!

WE DID.

VENUS, DO AN OLD STANDARD!

♪...I wish I knew how...to break the spell...I ought to say no-no-no, sir...

...at least I'm going to say that I trifled...

♪...I really can't stay ohh...but it's so cold outside...

⟨...BREATH-TAKING...⟩

⟨SHE'S... BEAUTIFUL...⟩

WOW. NO WONDER UNCLE MAKES HIS MEN WEAR THE EAR COVERS. SHE CAN'T BE STOPPED.

♪ BABY IT'S COLD OUTSIIIDE...

SO THESE AREN'T YELLOW CLAW'S BOYS?

NO, THEY'RE SOVIETS. SOME KGB OFFICER NAMED KARPOV IS PAYING FOR THE USE OF THE DRAGON'S CORRIDOR--WHAT YOU CAME THROUGH.

I WAS TO OVERSEE-- ENSURE THEY TRAVELED ONLY FOR THE OPERATION AGREED UPON.

BUT I WANTED TO SEE YOU AGAIN SO...I TOOK ONE OF THE MEN'S EMBLEMS.

THESE TRIANGLES DEFLECT RADIATION IN THAT CORRIDOR, DON'T THEY?

YES. AND SHOW YOU WHERE DOORWAYS ARE.

M-11, SCAN FOR ANYONE APPROACHING.

SO WHAT'S THE OPERATION THAT THE RUSSIANS NEEDED A SHORTCUT FOR?

UNCLE ONLY SAID THEY WERE STEALING CONTAINERS FROM THE FBI.

OVER HERE, I GOT THE REST OF IT FROM THIS MAN'S BRAIN. THE PARCELS ARE IN THAT BIG TRANSPORT.

HOLY--! THIS MiG HAS BELLS AND WHISTLES I'VE NEVER SEEN-- MUST BE A PROTOTYPE.

SAY, MARVEL BOY...DO YOU THINK THIS JET WILL GO THROUGH THAT CORRIDOR?

I GUESS IT COULD, KIT.

DON'T DROOL ON THE GLASS, SON.

I CAN'T IMAGINE WHAT THEY WANT FROM THE BUREAU. I'D THINK THEY'D USE THE CORRIDOR TO RAID LABS, OR AEROSPACE...

PROBABLY LOOKIN' FOR HOOVER'S COMIC BOOKS. BUT NOW WE'LL...

...SEE.

HOLY COW, IT-- IT'S...

INSIDE AMERICA

WRITER: JEFF PARKER
ARTIST: CLAYTON HENRY
COLORIST: JANA SCHIRMER
LETTERER: BLAMBOT'S NATE PIEKOS

NEW YORK CITY.

NOW.

--CAPTAIN AMERICA!

HRONNGH

NUTS!

M-11! TRY TO GRAB AHOLD OF THE CRANE OVER THERE!

...KEEP FALLING TOWARDS THE CONSTRUCTION SITE...GOOD.

KERRANG

Ugh, IF I HAVE TO HURL, I'M DOING IT ON HIM!

BOB! SORRY TO DO THIS WHEN YOU NEED REST, BUT WE'VE GOT A SITUATION.

OUR CLUE-SEEDING HAS WORKED TOO FAST.

WE COULD BLOW THE OPERATION BY ENGAGING TOO EARLY. NEED RETRIEVAL NOW!

ON... ON MY WAY...

KEN, WE NEED TO DISPOSE OF THE COPTER BEFORE WE TIP OUR HAT TOO SOON. GET HIM OFF OF IT.

Unf!

Oh--

--HAPPY TO!

DO YOU THINK THEY'RE ACTUALLY CAP AND BUCKY?

KIT, IT MAY NOT BE A GOOD IDEA TO TAKE THE JET BACK.

I'VE GOT TO TRY, MR. WOO. THE REDS MIGHT BE GETTING THE JUMP ON US IN AERO-SPACE.

I DON'T KNOW, BUT THE RUSSKIES DON'T HAVE ANY BUSINESS KEEPING THEM.

WE'VE GOT TO TAKE THE CORRIDOR BACK—I HOPE WE CAN FIND THAT SAME DOOR AGAIN.

HERE WHERE THE RADIO SHOULD BE...COULD BE A NEW MISSILE SYSTEM...

THAT IS A TARGETING INTERFACE. I THINK...YES. IT'S RELATED TO THE PORTAL GENERATOR WE CAME THROUGH.

I'D BET MY HEADBAND THAT THE JET IS EQUIPPED TO OPEN A PORTAL FOR ITSELF.

THAT'S WHERE YOU KEY IN LATITUDE AND LONGITUDE FOR YOUR DESTINATION. OF COURSE.

THEY BUILT IT GOING BY YELLOW CLAW'S MACHINE AND MUST HAVE THOUGHT SUWAN WAS LEAVING TO REPORT IT TO HIM.

ΘΔΘ
широта
38°53'23"N
77°00'27"W

IMAGINE THE SNEAK ATTACKS THEY COULD RUN WITH THIS GOING THROUGH THAT CORRIDOR!

RRRRRRRMMM

WHAT... JIMMY!

YOUR TRIP INTO THE SENTRY'S MIND DRAINED YOU...

...AND YOU PASSED OUT WHILE CONNECTING US. I THINK IF YOU TAKE OFF YOUR HEADBAND...

ARE YOU SUGGESTING THAT WE'RE TRAPPED IN A...

...LOOP?

LATER.

YOU SURE HE DIDN'T LEARN ANYTHING ABOUT OUR OPERATION?

HE NEVER VENTURED OUTSIDE HIS MEMORIES, BUT I WENT INTO HIS. HE'S NOT ONLY IN CONTACT WITH THE REAL AVENGERS, HE'S HIDING THEM.

PERFECT.

I LEFT THE INFORMATION YOU WANTED IN HIS MIND.

GOOD.

THEN IT'S TIME FOR THE SHOWDOWN.

"WE'RE ALMOST THERE! IF I GO ANY FASTER, WE'LL OVERSHOOT THE WHOLE VALLEY!"

AGENT WOO, YOUR GOVERNMENT ISN'T IN THE HABIT OF GIVING OUT SECRETS, EVEN WHEN IT'S GRATEFUL FOR YOUR WORK. WHICH WE ARE.

NOW HAS THE YOUNG MR. GRAYSON HERE HAD ANY LUCK WITH DUPLICATING THE EFFECT TO ENTER THAT CORRIDOR IN YOUR REPORT?

I MIGHT BE ABLE TO GET CLOSER IF YOU WOULD RETURN THE TRIANGLES YOUR MEN CONFISCATED.

TOO MUCH RISK NOT HAVING THOSE UNDER LOCK AND KEY.

ARE YOU SAYING YOU DON'T TRUST US, SIR?

YOU MAY BE DARLINGS OF PRESIDENT EISENHOWER, BUT YOU TAKE TOO MANY LIBERTIES WITH PROCEDURE FOR FBI STANDARDS, AGENT WOO.

I THINK WE'VE COME TO THE END OF THE USEFULNESS OF *DEPARTMENT ZERO*.

YOU'D THINK AT LEAST MY CHARMS WOULD HAVE HAD SOME EFFECT ON HIM.

DO YOU THINK THEY'RE REALLY GOING TO SHUT US DOWN?

HOOVER'S BEEN LOOKING FOR EXCUSES EVER SINCE WE STARTED. I THINK KIT'S DEATH FINALLY GAVE HIM THE ONE HE NEEDED.

IF HE DOES...

...THEN AMERICA JUST LOST ITS BEST AGENTS.

BROOKLYN, NEW YORK.

TODAY.

THEY'RE FORMIDABLE, HOW MUCH SO IS HARD TO SAY.

BUT THEY WERE ABLE TO GET INSIDE MY HEAD, WHICH MEANS THEY KNOW ABOUT *YOU.*

THEIR MUNITIONS FACTORY IS ON A SUPERTANKER ANCHORED NEARBY.

IF THE SOURCES I FOUND WERE RIGHT, THEY CAN ARM THOUSANDS OF OSBORN'S TROOPS WITH TECH BEYOND ANYTHING H.A.M.M.E.R. HAS YET.

NO TIME TO WASTE, THEN, AVENGERS.

SPIDER-MAN

LUKE CAGE

RONIN

WE'RE GOING OUT THERE TO BRING ATLAS *DOWN.*

MS. MARVEL

WOLVERINE

WOLVERINE

SPIDER-MAN

YOU KNOW OSBORN WILL PROBABLY JUST SPRING THESE GUYS TOMORROW, RIGHT?

THEN WE'LL BUST THEM AGAIN. AS LONG AS IT TAKES.

MS. MARVEL

I'LL GET THE OTHERS.

LUKE CAGE

RONIN

CAPTAIN AMERICA

...AVENGERS!

TAKING THE FALL

WRITER: JEFF PARKER   PENCILER: CARLO PAGULAYAN   INKER: JASON PAZ   COLORIST: JANA SCHIRMER   LETTERER: BLAMBOT'S NATE PIEKOS
COVER: BILLY TAN & FRANK D'ARMATA   VARIANT COVER: McGUINNESS, VINES & PONSOR   PRODUCTION: IRENE LEE
ASSISTANT EDITOR: LAUREN SANKOVITCH   SENIOR EDITOR: MARK PANICCIA   EDITOR IN CHIEF: JOE QUESADA
PUBLISHER: DAN BUCKLEY   EXECUTIVE PRODUCER: ALAN FINE

SO LET'S SEE JUST WHAT THEY'RE BRINGIN' THE OS-*BUM*.

RRNNNNK

THIS IS IT-- SOPHISTICATED ANTI-TECH WEAPONRY.

WHILE I WAS CONNECTED TO THE ONE WITH THE SPACE SUIT, I SAW A WHOLE FACTORY FOR THESE INSIDE THAT SHIP.

A MOBILE FACTORY? THIS ATLAS GROUP MUST HAVE SERIOUS RESERVES.

CAN I SEE ONE OF THOSE?

CAUGHT THESE TWO. ANYONE WANT TO WEB THEM FOR ME?

SHE MEANS YOU.

Mmm... Huh? OH YEAH.

SO THEY'VE GOT SOME ROBOT AND A GORILLA? SHOULDN'T BE HARD.

I GOT THE IMPRESSION OF OTHERS, TOO.

SOME RED-HAIRED WOMAN. I DON'T KNOW WHAT SHE DOES. THE OTHER WOMAN I RECOGNIZED FROM THE NEWS AROUND HULK'S INVASION.

SHE'S AN ATLANTEAN-HUMAN LIKE NAMOR. WITH ALL THE POWER YOU'D EXPECT.

WELL, GREAT.

IF THIS SHIPMENT IS AS BIG AS THEY SAY, WE'RE GOING TO HAVE TO CALL IN TWO MORE TRUCKS.

HOLD UP, GRIZZLY.

Oh HELL. THE AWOL AVENGERS ARE ONTO THE DEAL.

ARE YOU GOING TO GO HELP ATLAS?

DO I LOOK THAT STUPID, HODGES? I'M CALLING THIS IN TO OSBORN.

"ALL THE WORKERS ARE EVACUATED EXCEPT FOR THE ONES THEY JUST CAUGHT."

THEY'VE BUSTED OUR THUGS.

THERE WAS NO REFORMING THOSE GUYS--JAIL IS BEST FOR THEM.

NOT BAD, JIMBO. YOU'VE GOT ALL THE PIECES IN PLACE.

EXCEPT BOB, HE'S TOO WIPED OUT FROM YESTERDAY.

WHERE'S MY SILK--

HERE, EVIL MASTER.

THANKS.

I SEE NO POINT IN THIS RUSE. ALL OF THIS ARTIFICE TO LET YOURSELF BE BEATEN?

IS THE POINT TO MAKE ATLAS LOOK WEAK?

WHY DON'T YOU GO IN THE BACK AND *CHANNEL YOUR CHI* SOME MORE, BALDY.

NO, TEMUGIN, THE POINT IS TO *NOT* DELIVER ON THE WEAPONRY THAT OSBORN WANTED FOR H.A.M.M.E.R., AND TO HAVE A PLAUSIBLE REASON.

WE'VE DEVELOPED A RELATIONSHIP WITH OSBORN THAT HE BELIEVES AND IT'S YIELDED SOME GOOD INFORMATION.

NEVER HAVE I FOUGHT WITH LESS THAN MY ALL!

I WAS CAUGHT UNAWARE LAST NIGHT, BUT I HAVE SPENT THE DAY IN MEDITATION. I AM READY TO ENGAGE AN ARMY.

YOU ARE FREE TO FIGHT AT FULL CAPACITY--ANY LESS WOULD BLOW THE OPERATION.

BUT WITH BOB OUT, YOU ARE GOING TO BE A KEY PLAYER TODAY. YOU *MUST* FOLLOW MY PLAN.

BRING IT, KONG!

WATCH OUT FOR THE ROBOT'S ARMS!

M-11, TAKE CAGE. KEN--

RARGH!

MS. MARVEL IS MINE!

WAIT!

SPIDER, WHAT IN HELL ARE YOU--

EVERYONE STOP!

SO WHAT-- ARE YOU SAYING THEY **WANT** US TO DESTROY THIS FACTORY AND RUN THEM IN?

IF THEY WANTED TO ATTACK US, THEY COULD HAVE DONE IT WITH THE ELEMENT OF SURPRISE WHEN WE WERE SITTING DUCKS.

MASTER WOO...

AH... OKAY.

MAYBE WE SHOULD LEVEL WITH YOU.

JIMMY... YOU SURE?

RUN VOICE ANALYSIS...

AUDIO COMPARISON: 1958 CUBA MISSION...

(((So what--are you saying they want us to destroy this factory and run them in?)))

(((Figured you'd say something like that, G-Man. But that's not how my bosses like to play it.)))

VOICE ANALYSIS...

(((So what--are you saying they want us to destroy this factory and run them in?)))

TOO BAD BOB ISN'T HERE, IT'D BE EASIER FOR HIM JUST TO SHOW YOU.

THE ATLAS FOUNDATION USED TO BE RUN BY THE **YELLOW CLAW**--HE DIED RECENTLY.

SHOW US WHAT?

I DIDN'T REALIZE IT BUT HE'D ALWAYS PLANNED ON ME BECOMING THE NEXT LEADER...

Voice Match... **OPERATIVE LOGAN**...

TEK

WHOA-- FAST--

BZAAK BZAAK BZAAK

WMFFF

BUT NOT THIS FAST.

AHH--

KRANNG

AWAY FROM MASTER WOO.

WHOOGH!

DO I PLAY MY PART WELL, MASTER?

YOU DO.

COME ON V, TIME TO WRAP THIS UP...

WHERE'S THE ONE WHO WENT IN MY HEAD?!

KNNHH--!

TWUUNNG

EYYAAH!

YOU PUNK-- I'M GONNA FEED YOU THIS STICKY CRAP! COME BACK HERE!

I BET YOU'RE THE FOUR HUNDRED POUND GORILLA IN EVERY ARGUMENT--

BUT I GOTTA SEE ABOUT YOUR SNEAKY FRIEND.

NEXT: JOURNEY TO THE DEEP!

CLASSIFIED DOCUMENT / FEDERAL BUREAU OF
INVESTIGATION

CASE 7-A / JAMES WOO- HEAD OF WEST COAST SPECIAL
DEPARTMENT ZERO

Transcribed by Agent Angela Wellington,
San Francisco Adjunct

May 3rd, 1958/ CUBA

CLASSIFIED

As with all other transcriptions of Agent Woo's DEPART-
MENT ZERO group, I have received audio recordings from
the automaton known as M-11, supplemented with ac-
counts from the other members of the team. This was
particularly necessary in this instance as M-11's files
are exceptionally unreliable near mission's end, for
causes which will become apparent. Also supplied is
aerial photography from Bob Grayson's craft The Silver
Bullet.

-A. Wellington

THE JUNGLES OF CUBA. 1958.

LOGAN! ⇒zZzzZzhhht⇐ HAS HENDRICKS TURNED UP YET?

NO WORD FROM HIM.

FROM WHAT I CAN TELL, THE REVOLUTIONARIES DON'T HAVE 'IM. THEY'RE CONCERNED WITH SOME FLY-BY.

THE BIGWIGS ARE THERE, THOUGH.

I'M DOWNWIND, SO I CAN CIRCLE AROUND IF I HAVE TO.

YOU'RE RUNNING OUT OF TIME-- ⇒zzZzzhhht⇐ --BE OUT OF THERE BY ZERO-EIGHT-HUNDRED.

ALL RIGHT THEN, I'M GOING IN.

LOGAN OUT.

SNIFF SNIFF

THINK YA GOT THE DROP ON ME? FORGET IT!

I KNOW YOU'RE THERE!

M-11, THE HUMAN ROBOT.

RIGHT ANSWER! JIMMY, WHAT DOES PROFESSOR VAN DOREN WIN?

AN AIRLIFT BACK TO THE STATES AND FBI INTERROGATION IF HE CAN'T EXPLAIN WHAT HE'S DOING HERE.

JIMMY WOO, FIELD LEADER.

KEN HALE, CODENAME: GORILLA MAN.

WOLVERINE
AGENT OF ATLAS

WORDS—JEFF PARKER   ART—BENTON JEW
COLORS—ELIZABETH DISMANG BREITWEISER
LETTERS—BLAMBOT'S NATE PIEKOS
PRODUCTION—RANDALL MILLER
ASST. EDITORS—COSBY & SANKOVITCH
EDITOR—MARK PANICCIA
EDITOR IN CHIEF—JOE QUESADA
PUBLISHER—DAN BUCKLEY

PARDON MY CYNICISM, PAL, BUT YOU DON'T LOOK LIKE ANY OF HOOVER'S MEN I EVER SEEN.

AND YOUR WALKING FURNACE CAN FORGET TRYING TO LAY THAT MITT ON ME.

HEY!

≥NNK≥

Whoa! NOT BAD...

...BUT YOU GOTTA MO--

OOF!

SHUT UP.

CRUNNGH

WHO WERE YOU TALKING TO ON THAT TWO-WAY?

THE YELLOW CLAW?

WHY IS A CHINESE GUY ASKING *ME* IF I'M FRIENDLY WITH YELLOW CLAW?

DON'T GET SMART.

ξRRRKξ

WE'VE GOT A TIP THAT HE HAS AN OPERATION RUNNING DOWN HERE, AND IT LOOKS LIKE YOU'RE TRYING TO GET INVOLVED WITH THE STRUGGLE

ARE YOU A SPY OR--

HEY, YA SLIPPERY LITTLE--!

JIMMY!

RRARRH!

ZZZAK

M-11, STOP!

HE DIDN'T HURT ME, KEN. IT LOOKS LIKE HE WAS GOING FOR THIS...BUG?

WOW, THAT WAS ON MY NECK AND I DIDN'T EVEN FEEL IT!

Ah...NUTS, JIMMY. M-11 GAVE THE GUY A SEAT IN THE ELECTRIC CHAIR.

POOR LUG. LET'S AT LEAST MAKE HIS LAST ACT COUNT FOR SOMETHING.

HEY BOB, COME IN. WE'VE GOT SOMETHING FOR YOUR LAB.

A STRANGE INSECT? SEND IT UP IN M-11'S SAMPLE POD AND I'LL RUN IT THROUGH THE *SILVER BULLET'S* MINI-LAB.

DO YOU THINK IT'S CONNECTED TO THE YELLOW CLAW PLOT WE UNCOVERED?

ON ITS WAY.

I HOPE SO, VENUS, OR A MAN DIED FOR NOTHING.

≷KOFF≷ AS MARK... TWAIN SAID...

...≷KOFF≷ I FORGET WHAT THE HELL TWAIN SAID. BUT I AIN'T DEAD.

NO WAY. DIDN'T THINK SOME SCHMO COULD LIVE THROUGH *THAT* MUCH JUICE!

I'M GLAD YOU DID. SORRY, M-11 USED TO BE A KILLER ROBOT.

USED TO BE?

YOU DON'T SEE ANY OF THOSE BUGS ON *ME*, DO YA?

NO, YOU'RE CLEAR.

SO MISTER... LOGAN, CAN YOU TELL US WHAT THOSE *THINGS* ARE?

PART OF WHAT I'M DOWN HERE CHECKING OUT. THEY'VE BEEN TURNING UP ON KEY FIGURES IN THIS WHOLE REVOLUTION SHINDIG, AND THE SOURCE IS SOMEWHERE OUT HERE.

I'M FOLLOWING UP A PREVIOUS AGENCY TEAM WHO CHUTED IN LAST WEEK.

WHO'S IN ON THIS? C.I.A.? THE MILITARY?

FINE, DON'T ANSWER.

YOUR BUDDY'S FLYOVER HAS THE REBEL FORCES SPOOKED, THEY'RE MOVING OUT.

THEY MUST THINK BOB'S ROCKET IS A MISSILE.

HANG ON...

THAT'S HENDRICKS' SIGNAL, HE'S STILL ALIVE! HE LED THE FIRST TEAM.

HANG ON, PAL, I'M COMIN'.

SORRY TO INTRUDE, BUT WE'RE COMING TOO--IT LOOKS LIKE WE'RE ON THE SAME TRAIL.

M-11, CLEAR A PATH.

I PREFER STEALTH, BUT THAT WORKS.

Y'KNOW, I GOT A HYPOTHESIS ABOUT THIS SITUATION...

EE, I'M THINKIN' THESE UGS ARE LIKE LITTLE SSASSINS, INJECTING OW-ACTING OISON.

IT'S A ITTLE OUT THERE, I KNOW.

BUT A GORILLA SPOUTING THE THEORY IS PERFECTLY NORMAL.

THERE'S HENDRICKS, HE LOOKS OKAY.

FIGURED THEY'D SEND YOU, LOGAN.

ARE THESE NEW... AGENTS?

THEY'RE F.B.I. WHERE'S YOUR TEAM?

IF YOU DON'T RESIST, YOU'LL LIVE. LET THE SMALL ONES ATTACH, THEY WILL FEED YOUR CORTEX.

NUTS TO THAT!

SNAP OUT OF IT, HENDRICKS! YOU'RE DRUGGED!

NNH!

BLAM

RETURNING THE FAVOR!

LOOK OUT!

RRUNCH

MARVEL BOY TO JIMMY WOO, OVER. URGENT MESSAGE!

THAT BUG WAS STRUCTURALLY ALTERED TO DELIVER A PROTEIN SEQUENCE TO A HOST'S BRAIN!

WHAT IN IKE'S NAME DOES THAT MEAN, BOB?!

IT MEANS *MIND CONTROL,* KEN. DON'T LET ONE ATTACH TO YOU, THE PROCESS IS IRREVERSIBLE EVEN BY MY URANIAN TECHNOLOGY!

THAT'S ENOUGH FOR ME. EVERYONE FALL BACK BUT M-11!

DEATH RAY, BUDDY!

VOOOOOOSH!

BETTER THAN DDT.

EXCEPT HE MISSED ONE THING.

SORRY, HENDRICKS.

CRHCK

SEVERAL HOURS LATER...

THAT'S ENOUGH SEARCHING. AGENT LOGAN IS LONG GONE, IF THAT WAS REALLY HIS NAME.

POOR M-11. CAN YOU FIX HIM, BOB?

SURE, VENUS, I'VE BEEN MEANING TO OVERHAUL HIM FOR MONTHS. I'VE GOT SOME IDEAS FOR A GOOD REBUILD.

HIS "BRAIN" IS INTACT, THAT'S THE MAIN THING.

PATCH HIM UP GOOD, HE TOOK OUT THE CREEPIEST THREAT THE YELLOW CLAW HAS WHIPPED UP YET.

PERMANENT MIND-CONTROL...

"...JUST IMAGINE WHAT HE COULD HAVE DONE WITH THAT."

THE END.

PDX INTERNATIONAL AIRPORT.

--AGAIN WE REMIND YOU THAT CURRENT TRAVEL IS LIMITED TO CONVEYING FOOD OR SUPPLIES. ALL EARTH FLIGHT IS PROHIBITED.

ALL BROADCAST FREQUENCIES AND DATASTREAMS ARE NOW UNDER OUR CONTROL AS WELL.

ANY AGGRESSION WILL BE MET WITH RETALIATION.

PARKER RD
ONE NIGHT
ONLY

WE DO NOT WISH TO USE FORCE. PLEASE SURRENDER YOUR WEAPONS THAT WE MAY MAKE THIS TRANSITION AS PEACEFUL AS POSSIBLE.

THERE IS NO NEED TO FEAR THE GAS THAT OUR UNITS ARE SPRAYING. IT IS ONLY A SEDATIVE AGENT TO BE USED UNTIL RIOTING IS MINIMAL.

WE HAVE SECURED THE THREAT!

THE OCCUPATION OF THE NORTH AMERICAN WEST COAST WAS PROCEEDING ON SCHEDULE. PORTLAND, OREGON LACKED THE TERRESTRIAL DEFENSES OF OTHER METROPOLITAN CENTERS.

THE RESISTANCE

THE ONE WHO KILLED SUPER-SKRULL ALPHA! OUR ANALYSIS FOUND THAT SHE IS AN ATLANTEAN HYBRID, VULNERABLE TO DEHYDRATION.

GOOD WORK. DISPLAY HER THROUGH THE CITY TO SEND THE MESSAGE: DO NOT RESIST.

THANKS TO THOROUGH GOVERNMENT REGISTRATION, OUR ADVANCE TEAMS HAD SOLID INTELLIGENCE ON WHAT SUPERHUMAN THREATS TO EXPECT.

STILL, SOME OF THEIR DEFENSES HAD MANAGED TO STAY UNDETECTED.

AS THE GAS TAKES EFFECT, YOU MAY LEAVE YOUR WEAPONS WITH THE ARMS COLLECTOR AND RETURN TO YOUR HOMES.

YOU TWO! PROCEED NO FURTHER!

HOW ARE YOU RESISTING THE GAS?!

GAS MASK. Oh, Duh. I FORGET...

...YOU GUYS THINK YOU CORNERED THE MARKET ON SHAPE-CHANGING.

KRAK

I NOW KNOW THESE SUBVERSIVE AGENTS AS THE RULING COUNCIL OF A VAST UNDERGROUND NETWORK. **THE ATLAS FOUNDATION.** OUR PARANOIA CAMPAIGN SUCCESSFULLY CUT THEM OFF FROM THOSE FORCES, AS IT HAS WITH OTHER CHAMPIONS. THEY DO NOT KNOW WHO TO TRUST.

THEIR GROUND GENERAL IS KEN HALE, A MAN TRANSFORMED BY AN ANCIENT CURSE TO BECOME THE **"GORILLA MAN."** HE IS WELL VERSED IN BATTLE AND PLANNING.

M-11! GET HER HYDRATED, **NOW!**

THEIR SENTIENT ANDROID IS DESIGNATED M-11, SOMETIMES CALLED THE **HUMAN ROBOT** FOR REASONS I HAVE YET TO LEARN.

HE SPEAKS RARELY AND IS HARD TO FATHOM.

UNLIKE THE ONE CALLED **NAMORA.**

SHE IS OF THE SAME PHYSIOLOGY AS THE ATLANTEAN KING NAMOR. HIS FORCES WERE SUCCESSFULLY DISPERSED THROUGH MANIPULATION, BUT WE DID NOT EXPECT TO ENCOUNTER ANOTHER HYBRID OF HIS STATURE.

EEYAA!

THE EMPIRE SAW LITTLE TACTICAL ADVANTAGE IN THE AREA, AND AS A RESULT WE WERE ILL-PREPARED FOR SUCH A COUNTERATTACK. THIS IS HOW I WAS CAPTURED.

HALE INNATELY RECOGNIZED MY STANDING AS A LEADER AMONG THE GROUND FORCE, THOUGH I BELIEVE HE HADN'T EXPECTED TO ACQUIRE A FIELD MARSHAL.

GOT BOB'S SPECIMEN, LET'S CLEAR OUT!

WE'VE ALREADY BEEN HERE TOO LONG!

I'LL HEAD SOUTH AND WE'LL COME BACK UP TO THE SAUCER THROUGH THE RIVER.

YOU PUNKS DON'T BREATHE WATER, SO I'D WEAR THIS.

MRPHH!

THE TEAM HAD PICKED A PERFECT HIDING PLACE FOR THEIR SAUCER. COMING FROM THE ARID SKRULL WORLDS, WE WOULD NOT THINK TO SCAN THE BOTTOM OF THE RIVER.

IT WAS BUILT BY THE HUMAN BOB GRAYSON, FORMERLY **MARVEL BOY**. HIS HUMANITY IS MOSTLY APPEARANCE, AS HIS BODY WAS ALTERED PROFOUNDLY TO LIVE WITH NATIVE URANIANS AT THE CORE OF THE SEVENTH PLANET.

I HOPE THIS THING WORKS.

GRAYSON IS AS EFFICIENT AS OUR SCIENTIST AND HAS TECHNOLOGY EVEN WE LACK. HIS HEADBAND HAS SCANNED MY MIND FOR MILITARY SECRETS, AND IN DOING SO, HE'S ALLOWED ME ACCESS TO THEIR OWN. WHAT I KNOW COULD COMPROMISE THIS TEAM GREATLY.

IT WILL.

OF COURSE, I NOW HAVE NO WAY OF SENDING THIS INFORMATION. EVEN AS MY VOCAL CORDS HANG DISCONNECTED.

I LIKE TO THINK EVE ROYAL BIOLOGISTS W NOT LEAVE A SPECIA HEAD WHERE IT CO WATCH ITS OWN VIVIS

TKK-THMMM

THEY'VE FOUND US! SURFACE THE SAUCER WITH ONE-WAY SHIELD!

BOB, IS THAT READY TO GO?

YES. VENUS AND I WILL MEET YOU UP TOP.

THE ONE CALLED **VENUS** IS LITERALLY FROM THE HUMANS' WESTERN MYTHOLOGY, THOUGH NOT WHAT HER NAME SUGGESTS. SHE IS PERHAPS A THOUSAND YEARS OLD.

MOST OF HER EXISTENCE WAS AS A SEASIDE DWELLER KNOWN AS A SIREN, OR NAIAD. SHE LATER REINVENTED HERSELF AS A CHAMPION OF PEACE AND LOVE.

THEY HAVE A **FORCE WALL!**

THEY'RE PUSHING THE SHIELD BACK, IT'S NOT GONNA LAST!

HOLD YOUR FIRE! BOB AND VENUS NEED TO DO THEIR THING.

USING THIS BRAIN IN A CIRCUIT WITH MY HEADBAND, SHE'LL BE ABLE TO HIT THE SPECIFIC HARMONICS TO AFFECT THEM.

haskk... shness... kak..

IN TRUTH, SHE IS THE DEADLIEST OF THE AGENTS.

THE POWER OF HER SONG IS OVERWHELMING. WITH NO BODY STILL I FELT ITS EFFECT.

MY REGIMENT HAD NO DEFENSE AGAINST IT, THEY COULD ONLY BE DRAWN TO THE SOURCE.

YET EVEN AS THE ENEMY HAD THE VICTORY, I FELT A REPRIEVE FROM THE VOICE. VENUS HAD STOPPED.

I CAN'T DO IT, JIMMY. IT'S JUST LIKE WITH THE SAILORS...

THEY'RE NOT EVIL.

WHAT?

IT'S TRUE. THIS MIND SHOWS NO MALEVOLENCE. IT'S NOT JUST PROPAGANDA--THEY MEAN TO BRING US INTO THEIR SOCIETY FREE OF WAR AND INJUSTICE.

THEY BELIEVE IT'S OUR DESTINY TO BE ONE CIVILIZATION. WITHOUT SUFFERING.

THE LAST MEMBER IS JAMES WOO. OUR FILES SHOW HE WORKED FOR S.H.I.E.L.D. UNTIL RECENTLY.

I WON'T MAKE YOU DO IT, V. AND I BELIEVE YOU, BOB.

I KNOW I SEEM LIKE A THROWBACK... ALL OF YOU WENT ON WITH YOUR LIVES SINCE WE WERE FIRST A TEAM, AND I'M STRAIGHT OUT OF 1958.

WOO WAS CRITICALLY INJURED, THEN RESCUED BY HIS ORIGINAL TEAM. GRAYSON RESTORED HIM TO HIS YOUNGER SELF.

EVEN IF OUR INTELLIGENCE HAD BEEN CURRENT, HE WOULD HAVE BEEN OVERLOOKED. OUR STATISTICIANS WOULD HAVE FOCUSED ON HIS EXTRAORDINARY TEAMMATES.

HECK, MAYBE THEY DO WANT TO SAVE US FROM OURSELVES. MAYBE THE WORLD WOULD BE A BETTER PLACE.

YET HE HAS THE GREATEST POWER OF ALL.

BUT FROM WHERE I STAND...

...THOSE ARE GREEN MEN FROM OUTER SPACE TRYING TO TAKE OVER THE EARTH. M-11?

DEATH RAY.

THE ABILITY TO LEAD.

I AM MUTE WITNESS TO A GROWING UNDERGROUND MOVEMENT. OUR YEARS OF PLANS ARE BASED ON THE HUMAN TENDENCY TO BRASH ACTION.

BOB, TAKE US TO SEATTLE.

WE'LL DO WHAT WE CAN THERE, AND THEN IT'S BEST TO MOVE OUT OF THE U.S. FOR A WHILE. JAPAN NEXT.

LOOK AT THIS FORMATION.

I KNOW A SECT OF ATLANTEANS NOW IN THE NORTHERN PACIFIC WHO CAN BE TRUSTED TO HELP...

NOW THE TERRANS ARE RESORTING TO SUBTERFUGE. THEY ARE FIGHTING US...

...LIKE SKRULLS.

END

KIRK (AFTER KIRBY)

...and that is certainly *Captain America.*

CAPTAIN AMERICA

STORM

IRON MAN

SPIDER-MAN

GIANT-GIRL

WOLVERINE

THE **AVENGERS**

JIMMY WOO

VENUS

GORILLA MAN

MARVEL BOY

NAMORA

AGENTS OF **ATLAS**

M-11, THE HUMAN ROBOT

RUN!

HEELLLLP!

The report was true!

AVENGERS ASSEMBLE!

Giant-Girl, run around the block and cut them off. We need to halt the stampede.

I can corral one of them.

So what do we do with this hole?

Nothing, apparently. It looks to be closing on its own.

All right, that's a wrap! Let's go get lunch.

That would be nice, Spider-Man, but we need to find out how tyrannosaurs are making 30-million-year leaps through time.

Maybe they're just really cool?

Why's the tin man acting like he just scored the winning touchdown?

It takes a lot of energy to open such a vortex in the dimension of time. Energy that gives a specific signal.

Whatever caused that temporal hole has to be in the area.

There! The source is hanging just out of synch with our progression of time.

It feels like a meteorological anomaly does.

Excellent detecting, Iron Man. Then I shall phase nearer to your time-stream so you may behold the glory...

I believe Iron Man has equipment that may alert you all to Time/Space manipulations affecting you directly.

And I do.

So I needed to give you a chore while the Kang of 3066 sent a message for me.

Ah, what good timing.

Hello, Kang.

Kang.

The super-team of 1958 has taken the message. The timeline will adjust accordingly soon.

What super-team of 1958?

Cap! You were around back then! Do you remember any other super heroes?

I was still frozen in the Arctic at that point, until the first roster of Avengers thawed me out.

Precisely. You've led this team to greatness, always interfering with my plans.

So I thought, what if you had been found sooner?

History flows in very specific ways and is actually quite difficult to alter.

Lasting changes can only be initiated by inhabitants of the time period, or time will soon correct itself.

For example, the timeline would only accept Captain America's return carried out by a super-team such as your-selves. My studies revealed such an earlier group.

"...into *their* time."

Is it really him?

The last time he was seen was on a plane that crashed up in these waters, so I guess it could be.

M-11...

...set your eyebeam low enough...

...to melt that ice!

Where... where am...

...I?

Captain America, welcome to 1958.

Oh, that was very tragic. My instruments had detected a meteor racing towards Earth.

They set out to destroy it, like the noble heroes they were. But the celestial object had defied all readings, even Marvel Boy's.

It turned out to be a travelling black hole, that pulled our friends in. I was able to redirect it, but...painful memories.

Better times ahead, eh?

WE ♥ KANG!

No!

You people are violating the Secret Identities Act.

You'll have to come with us.

The vortex...

...it's electrical...

Let go!

Kang is a criminal from the future!

Right, sir. Now come on...

I can affect it...

Hey Storm! Storm!

Excuuuussse mee...can I have your attenn-tionnn...

MMmmmm...hmm-hmmm mmmmmm...

Thanks, V. Okay, folks...

...I'm guessing there's more to this than some sneak attack. Let's palaver.

Palaver?

Isewhere...

What a freak accident!

Thanks for saving us from that broken train-trestle, Mr. Kang!

Indeed. Now I must go...

...and create perils for the next 54 decades that require my help.

Kang! Come in, Kang!

Kang, help! We're under att-- ZZZHHH--

Attack? Marvel Boy, do you hear me.

Blast!

Fah! All these interruptions when I'm so close!

The Avengers?!

We're going to expose your plans to the people of 1958!

I don't know how you defeated the Agents, but I have the public on my side already.

They'll never believe you, I'm the beloved Kang who brought back their Captain America!

See, Ken, the Avengers are on the level.

Then what are we waitin' for?

No! War Chariot, defend me!

Marvel Boy, get his headpiece!

Got it, Storm!

Thanks, M-11!

A machine is nothing before a Monarch of the Sea! Don't take that personally, M-11.

Trying to give us the slip?

Nuts! I've always wanted to hit Kang!

Secretly.

This could be a trick!

You have to trust us, it isn't his time to come back yet!

How could bringing back Cap make things go wrong?

Hey!

Everybody in the future turns out to be a bunch of runts!

You better put me *down!*

Heh, that was me all right.

It seemed like us. It's your call, Jimmy.

WOLVERINE ART APPRECIATION VARIANT BY GERALD PAREL

SECRET INVASION: WHO DO YOU TRUST? 2ND-PRINTING VARIANT

FRONT FIGURES
IN FULL COLOR

ENTIRE BACKGROUND MONOCHROME
IN A COLOR THAT
BEST SUITS THE
CHARACTER
EX. VENUS — PINK

STATS OF THE OTHER
TEAM MEMBERS IN
BACKGROUND